Why did the old Persians hold the sea holy? Why did the Greeks
give it a separate deity, and own brother Jove? Surely all this is
not without meaning. And still deeper the meaning of that story
of Narcissus, who because he could not grasp the tormenting mild
image he saw in the fountain, plunged into it and was drowned.
But that same image, we ourselves see in all rivers and oceans.
It is the image of the ungraspable phantom of life, and this is the
key to it all.

~**From** *Moby Dick* **by Herman Melville**

Ourselves in Rivers and Oceans
a poetry anthology

Edited & curated by
Claire Thom, Marc Brimble,
John Tessitore & Sarah Jeannine Gawthrop
for
The Wee Sparrow Poetry Press

Cover photograph © Mike Curry

Logo illustration © Colin Thom

Cover layout & manuscript formatting by Stuart Beveridge

Proofread by Katherine E Winnick

ISBN 978-84-09-57442-1 (paperback)

Ourselves in Rivers and Oceans

A Poetry Anthology

About The Cover Photograph

Professional photographer Mike Curry kindly gave us permission to use one of his photographs on the front cover of this anthology.

Mike Curry, a photographer for over forty years, navigates the realms of abstract photography with a unique focus on water as his muse. Inspired by the fluidity, reflections, and distortions found especially in urban aquatic environments, Curry crafts mesmerizing compositions that challenge conventional perceptions.

In Mike Curry's lens, water becomes a dynamic canvas, capturing the interplay of light and shadow, creating ethereal abstractions that transcend the ordinary. His work invites viewers to explore the beauty in the unseen, encouraging a deeper connection with the elemental forces that surround us.

The cover photograph by Mike Curry encapsulates the essence of his abstract approach—a plastic bag suspended in water. This seemingly mundane object transforms into a visual symphony of form and colour. The photograph belies its everyday origin, transcending the banal and elevating the plastic bag to an object of contemplation and beauty. Curry's ability to find art in the ordinary, especially in the environmental context, underscores his commitment to raising awareness about the fragile balance between humanity and nature.

Through his abstract explorations in water, Mike Curry invites us to reconsider the overlooked and discover the profound in the seemingly trivial, fostering a renewed appreciation for the intricate dance between elements in our world.

Contents

Foreword

Water fills me with wonder. I feel woven by threads of water, myth and ancestry, and I feel the hum of saltwater in my veins. I was born in Ireland, an island nation in the North East Atlantic where rock and sea collide in Donegal Bay. This is a place where even though water was holy, the sea remained a place of loss and leave-takings for centuries. I am named after a wave at a river mouth that is, in turn, named after the salmon that used to run the river in abundance. My birth place and home is in the catchment of a unique coastal lagoon where, despite its protected status, the quality of the water continues to decline year on year.

The collection of poems in *Ourselves in Rivers and Oceans* captures this dynamic, entangled and oftentimes messy relationship we have with water. Water is a shapeshifter cycling through the Earth's systems and changing climate, becoming vapour, solid, liquid or gas. Transforming into mist, cloud, rain, snow, glacier, aquifer, lake, dew, spring, creek, rivers over land, delta, estuary, ocean, rivers underground, and even rivers in the sky. It touches everything and is changed by everything that touches it. The environment that water finds itself in alters its structure, leaving an imprint of where it has been and all that it has experienced.

Despite the story of all life beginning with water, our relationship with water is broken. In today's modern society, much of our water bodies, rivers and seas have become degraded, polluted and silenced and we have forgotten how to listen to them. Emphasised in the writings of many indigenous and black feminist scholars and activists, such as John Mohawk and Christina Sharpe, and echoed in many of the poems in this anthology, there is a direct and powerful connection between the conquest and oppression of Indigenous people and other minorities (especially women) and the conquest of water. "Everywhere water/ Yet creation thirsts", writes Alison Sesi in her poem 'Kakhovka Dam' in this anthology. This control and conquest of water is most painfully visible in the profanity of weaponising the vitality of water — contaminating and restricting the supply of water — in recent global conflicts and wars. This pervasive colonial narrative of dominance and superiority to the natural world has violently disrupted our natural entanglement and symbiotic relationship with water, leaving a trail of destruction.

The story of power and dominion over water does not serve us or the planet well. This anthology shares new ways of relating to water, and new stories of reconnection. The poems reveal the importance of a way of being with water that goes beyond a controlling and extractive interaction, instead embracing the value of bringing play, love and intention into that relationship. Water teaches us the power of presence, the value of feeling and being with all of who we are so that we may act with greater clarity and empathy.

Like the flow of the water cycle, renewing our relationship with water is a cyclical tale of rhythm and movement, giving and receiving, inhalation and exhalation, ebb and flow; where water is at the beginning and end of every cycle of life. Restoring our sacred relationship with water through poetry, ritual and restoration is essential if we are to heal the waters of the world and, because we are water, heal ourselves. As we learn to be more like water, we become more fluid in our responses and less reactive, no longer resisting but able to flow. Facts and figures may fail to move us, but there is great power in poetry that speaks to our emotions and intuition, allowing us to feel and igniting a spark in our bellies.

Reading this deeply immersive anthology, may you feel inspired to get to know your water and listen to it, cherish and protect it, and in turn to become known by the water and all that it gives life to. Our health and the health of this blue Earth depends on it.

Easkey Britton, PhD. Surfer, scientist, explorer and more.
Author of *Ebb & Flow, Saltwater in the Blood,*
and *50 Things to Do by the Sea.*

Boat Magic
By A G Parker

i.   Turn your boat widdershins until her nostrils flair in the wind.
(Do not mind if she sways and shivers on the waves;
she is readying herself.)
Ensure you have all parts required for this spell before you begin.
Step in,
maintain balance.
If you heart is too full, your rage too unencumbered,
you will be pulled toward the waves
and the marid who resides between them –
and perhaps you can wrestle it into submission,
gain a wish, but
best to remain in a state of equilibrium.

ii.   Hoist
her aluminium spire up
to the heavens. This is your cathedral now.
She will take your blood, skin
your knees, remind you
of freedom.

iii. Shoulder the burden of the boom-wrapped sail and imagine
all the days of angst and collared shirts and ties unfurl,
wind-strewn, released,
as you unroll and hoist the sail.
Take care to avoid these whipping memories
while the tac remains loose.

iv. Next, the jib.
Best to station yourself against the mast as you secure first
the second sail, then its sheets.
Thread, the right way, through the fairlead. Imagine your focus
is a prayer. Take
the end:
Make a head,
strangle it,
poke it in the eye.
Twice.

v. Lastly, you'll need something to keep you on course.
The wind is wild and will drag you onto the rocks
to join mermaids who sing.
            The tide, less jealous, is merely indifferent.
Insert the daggerboard. (If you do not have one, loose the centreplate.)
Attach, then, your rudder. Both pins.

vi. Whisper to your floating church your intention.
Everything, now, is intention.
Finally, release the bowline, leave the dock,
sail away. Feel the balance
of nature within the palms of your hands, the arch of your spine,
the stretch and strain of every fibre of rope and tissue
as you become one
with wind and waves.

Halfway Down the Water Slide
By Aaron Sandberg

I threw palms against the plastic,
splayed legs along the sides.

No lifeguard back then
to make sure we came out

all right in the end.
I took the shock

of the first kid
who took the brunt

of the one after him.
So on. And so on.

How simple-strong
the past was, is.

I still hear it. Can feel its
dumb strength now—

the world with all its
screaming lungs

and kicking feet
slowly building up behind.

In Memoriam; The Solomon Browne
(8.12pm 19th December, 1981)
By Abigail Ottley

Here's to the men of the Solomon Browne
Who left off their work and went down, down, down.
Down in the dark where they pushed out to sea,
Those stout-hearted seamen, the pride of Penlee.

And what risks they braved their coxswain knew
For he took one son but he wouldn't take two
That wild, black night when the waves rose so high
It seemed that the ocean would swallow the sky

And the Union Star saw the rocks loom black
As the lifeboat went in and would not be pushed back
For it fell to these men of the Solomon Browne
To put on their jackets and go down, down, down.

They gave all they had, these exceptional men.
They'd lifted off four when they went in again.
They went in again, though they must have known
the odds were high they would never go home.

But, Cornishmen all, they would not look away.
They answered the call when it sounded that day.
We've got four off, the coastguard heard.
Then came the silence. No more words.

Different Strokes
By Albert Mundane

The ducks on the pond flew up
and straight into grandpa's watercolour
where they have hung mid-flight above
the mantelpiece for over fifty years

Was down by the river last night;
a heron flew up and straight into my google drive
where it will hang with the rest of my shit
until the cows come home.

Kakhovka Dam
By Alison Sesi

The ground troops have not
Made ground enough.
Time to launch the flood offensive
Time to let water do the
Work of war
Water in its profound profanity
Of inherent danger and flowing filth:
Putinesque putrefaction
Yielding up corpses
From another war long past.

Everywhere water
Yet creation thirsts
Everywhere water
Yet the land will be desert
Everywhere water
Surrounds a church
Where the Creator's
Living water awaits,
Clean and cleansing:
In the baptismal font is held

Salvation

So unesteemed people
Can do great things, and
Every last animal
Non-partisan, helpless,
Innocent and ignorant of
The ways of men

Is rescued

From the unholiness
Unleashed by the
Doctrine of death.

Dark Nights For A Fisherman's Wife
By Amy Bingham

She felt assured when, in the past at night,
she'd sight his stream of white relieving light
with sides of green then red towards the pier
to guide his boat to harbour, starboard side -
another storm force beaten, just in time.

She'd always pray for safe returns each time
his vessel ventured off, both day and night,
and with his small but trusted crew on side,
their weathered years of skills would come to light
when telling tales of tough sails from the pier.

The couple's cottage looked out to the pier,
where she would often wait for tide and time
to spot his distant reassuring light,
which lit the waves of challenges at night
to steer him home to be beside her side.

She'd sometimes sense the risky seas outside
as strong winds battered windows, where she'd peer
through panes and pain to trawl the darkened night
with desperate eyes and mind, until such time
oppressive skies revealed his glowing light.

But then, one night, he dimmed their bedroom light
to darken dreams that rested by her side,
before he kissed her sleepy head, in time
to leave and catch the tide down by the pier
and sail into a hurricane that night.

That final night. No light would reappear
beside her side. The storm force won that time.

Reticent Rain
By Amy L Smith

Listen, silence is not a quiet land.
Around the world, flooding. Here,
a single raindrop dents the sand.

Essential oil of soil, this scent
pressed from rock by humid air –
listen, silence is not a quiet land.

The big dog hides from thunder's plan –
expectant tension thickens the air
as a flashing raindrop dents the sand.

Wind whips and whistles, a jazz band
riff, clouds shift with water's hesitant glare,
and listen, this silence is not a quiet land.

Sporadic sprinkles, their dance unplanned
a distant wind chime tinkles unaware,
as a ringing raindrop dents the sand.

Water dreams what the land withstands –
her deep bone ache of longing prayer.
Listen, this silence is not a quiet land
when a single raindrop dents the sand.

A Very Brunswick Xmas
By Anna Dean

Dreaming of Xmas
when we were young
on the banks
of the River Brunswick
playing in the shallows
as the tide went out
watching crabs
scuttle and fossick –

of our once-a-year
holiday camp
filled with laughter
games and cricket
and the sandy cove
across the bridge
where we christened
our masks and flippers –

of the fair in the park
as the axemen chopped
and fairy floss
melted on lips –

of fireworks exploding
as the day turned dark
and we munched
on fairground chips -

of the pirate ship
that lured us in
with its fleet of boats
we rowed upstream
swashbucklers
in our daydreams –

of the kids
we met every year
our forever holiday friends

who played
in our memories
all year long
'til Xmas came again –

dreaming of Xmas
when we were young
on the banks
of the River Brunswick
of sand and sun
and sea and fun
and our Xmas holiday
wish list.

Agnes & the Finman
By Anna Kisby

Our first swim. I hang back – he dives in,
flips off legs, shape-shifts and pulls me
under. I am tangled in flippers gill-kissed,
forget the protest of my bones, the shock-cold
of a North Sea that wakes for him and glitters
gold as pagan coins thrown into wells for wishes.
Even the virgin's-veil blue of the sky is on his side
for as we loop and star-shape, my feet touching fins,
the clouds unscroll, become terrible angels
beating vast wings, decreeing *Thou Shalt Love!*
and in such light I'll sign up blind to whatever religion
he is offering, swallow salt and be cured
by the stroke of his swim, by his selkie-skin,
say I do, blinking into the undoable knot of the sun.

Previously published in *All the Naked Daughters*, Against the Grain Press, 2017
& *Watermarks: writing by lido lovers and wild swimmers*, 2017

A Boat Trip
By Anna Quarendon

The Falcon and the Osprey leave the harbour,
ply the bay where the crocus yellow tender
bobs blue-rimmed at its quayside mooring.
And men, weathered by sun and sea spray
lean on railings the colour of cormorants
to watch the day's cargo of visitors.

Past the shocking pink of buoys that float
beside the orange lifeboat The Seahorse
rides the petrel grey out to the island,
surges forward as the spindrift leaps
to drench the navy rucksack
and liver spotted spaniel,

nose lifted to the screech of silvered gulls
out of reach in the late September sky
above the dark rocks where the shag
spreads its darker wings to dry,
she scatters his grey ashes
in diamond bright water.

At the Hammam
By Anne Macaulay

She beckons me in to the tiny hammam,
room only for one to sit – me.
I undress foolishly not knowing the form
as she stands barefoot in a simple shift
her black eyes smiling through the steam.
She points, (she has no English, I have no Arabic),
and I sit on the stone bench as required,
and succumb.
She dips a copper pot in the cauldron of water
and douses me, again and again.
Like a helpless child, I am soaped carefully, firmly.
Le savon noir est bon? Oui –
We nod and smile at these few shared words.
More water sluices over me, before
the scrubbing and scouring of all my flesh.
The copper pot cascades over and over
through the fragrant heat haze,
till doused and drowsed,
even softer and pinker,
I am born again.

Pond's Edge
By April Woody

The yellow-blazed trail passes by a manmade pond. Parallel planks span the muck at the water's edge. Salamanders swim through slimy blades and leaves. What looks like a milky substance floating among all this life turns out to be a reflection of clouds. On a submerged branch several fat tadpoles perch, tails jutting out, looking like birds.

underwater tree
the night sky
still finds it

River Whisper
By Ashley Reynolds

The river did not trickle slowly
behind tall pines
or wait calmly for my arrival.
She surged through summer days, watching
our fumbled movements through twisted creeks.
A maze of leaves, deep roots, rocks,
landed us breathless on her sandy bank.
Fleeing a mosquito haze in heat
that pressed our tender bodies
closer to the water's edge,
we danced nervous toes
into her swelling shores.
A slow submersion quickened
until it flowed full force.
We plunged into her rushing current,
fully submerged, adrift
the fleeting fever of young love.

The river's wandering beauty curved along,
until the dusk song of cicadas called us home.
Only the imprints of our naked feet
watched us leave.

How quietly they whispered
before washing away.

Fish Out of Water
By Brigid Johnson

Preparing to birth,
the nesting instinct kicks in.
Except this is no nest
and there are no kicks.

Around the taps, plughole
water flows and I scrub at scum clinging to bowl.
Smoothing wrinkled sheets,
the hoover sucks up
all it can find to
fill its fat belly.
Everywhere dust.

First come the slops –
a sudden gush like a burst sewer
spewing its contents onto grey tiled floor
leaving you stranded –
a fish without water

Stubborn, it's in the genes
you're hooked out
by the affable doctor with deft hands.
I see myself in her eyes:
small, white, lost at sea

my buoy

Afterwards we say goodbye
in the small room with
angels stencilled on bleached walls.
I force my eyes to look at what's
beached in a towel
and concentrate on staying afloat.
I am a whale and grief is my Jonah.
I swallowed him whole.

Even now, he takes me by surprise,
scraping my guts
squeezing my bones
flooding out of every pore;
so I pull myself up, gulp him back down
and swim on, swim on, swim on

I Grow Gills and Learn to Breathe Under Water

(A poem about bipolar.)

By Carella Keil

Warm memories like shimmering colored sands I sift through my palms, day after day, until the sun sets and the sands dry and darken, and instead of shaking the dirt off my palms, I sit and stare. At the dirt in my palms. And instead of making new memories, I rub my hands against the old, again and again, until every grain of sand loses its sparkle.

Rippling sheets of purple panic, swelling emotions. Ocean waves rush at me, crest, but refuse to crash. The tantalizing waves lure me in for a month. Every day I keep them at bay, scrambling further up the shore. I wonder which is worse, to drown in the Sand or the Sea?

Tonight, the moon is shaped like a letter-opener. I have words for you and the sky. The stars are tugging me, the sea sings, and the sand turns to glass. Exhaling a breath I've held for decades, I dance to the memory of fallen meteorites on glass shores.

A Glass of Water
By C M John

Tap-calm, gravity-drawn,
downhill, down pipe
from the neighbour's field

peat-stained, faint fell
memories; wild nights
of cloud-storm, Atlantic
rain bundled across
the Pennines; drained
through layers of rock,
of time

forced through fissures,
springs appear, disappear,
reappear; tumble down fields,
burrow through rush, a mess
of mud

our spring, flows faithful,
drought defying, fills our pond
pipes, troughs. Gurgles
into our house, clear, fresh.
No chlorine, but acidic; copper
blue sheen tracks its progress
across white ceramic. Pinhole
leaks its thirty-year legacy.

Another Winter in St. Petersburg
By Carol V. Davis

A man stepped off the embankment
            onto the ice
The river was not reliable
            but he trusted it
the way a couple plunges into love
            not knowing if it will last
February, the ice could crack under foot
            not surprising anyone
Assuredly he walked with certainty
            a kind of belief
He did not need an answer to know
            his prayer reached its destination
The wind swirled, tossing a confetti of snow
            onto the broad back of the river
He continued until out of sight
            Scouring the papers the next day
no mention of a man sliding under
            though over many nights
I saw one leg, then the other, his torso
            swallowed too, silently
as if nothing had happened

Previously published in *Below Zero*, Stephen F.
Austin State University Press, 2023

Brockhill Park, Sunday Afternoon
By Carolyn Oulton

A few feet away, the child is waiting.
Strands of rain, wind's pummelling,
salt sun (even a woman, bent
like a pause in conversation)
have left that day intact.

Today the day after that day
means tomorrow. I know at once
this is tomorrow. Grass that is almost
too green to be not quite pink,
a leaf glazed on the mudbank.

Lumpy stones trudge across the stream,
holding my foot as my body
slides like foam, water reaching
for my toes. Another moment -
I am climbing the arch of a tree.

No. Not that.
But I take off my watch,
prod a stick
in the direction of the sea.
Tell no one where I am.

After the storm
By Chris Barras

The sea leaves a trail of vomit
along the high tide mark
made from pollution, jetsam
let loose from mankind's
careless use of the sea

Seaweed is shaken loose
lies brittle, wind-dried
catching rope with sand
embedded in the twists

Snagging old plastic bottles
once clear and bright
now dull as cataracts.
Tired beach toys abandoned
lost, part digested.

Seafoam spittle, leaves
the taste of bile
dead sea birds and fish
caught in ghost tackle
is retched on to the beach
clearing her throat for a while.

Untitled
By Chris Langer

road puddles-
jumping into
old memories

Whirlpool
By Chris Wilson

"The washer's on the blink," you sigh with resignation,
Socks soaked in soapy water pooling over the laminate,
Like tears leaking without cessation,
The tea towel saturated: clearly inadequate.
I fetch the toolbox, confident of a solution:
"It's probably one of your hair clips blocking the drain,"
And you tut, arms folded, threatening retribution
As detergent bubbles in the drawer, barely contained.
The washer vibrates, pulling against the hose.
"It's stuck, I announce" tinkering the controls,
"Between a spin and rinse cycle, I suppose."
Then the water's drained in overflowing bowls.
"Watch it, you bloody idiot!" You chastise.
"I knew we should've called the repair man-"
"But they cost an absolute fortune," I advise,
"I can fix this. I can".
Yet, your incredulity suggests otherwise.
I dislodge the culprit, and without a plan
I opt to investigate further, certain there's more
To find, and press on without a pause to rest
And ignore as you implore
Harangue and protest.
After removing the back panel without due care,
Neglecting which screw or which washer goes where
I discover hidden rust from unseen leaks around the gasket,
Realising the exterior of the washer must have masked it.
And we survey years of damage, hands thrown up in despair,
We're left to conclude: it's finally beyond repair."

Kelp
By Ciarán Parkes

In his last email he describes kelp
growing taller than the tallest tree
and how Shackleton and his small crew,
seeking help from Elephant Island, knew

they could cling to it as a last resort
if they didn't make landfall before darkness
fell again and how the danger
wasn't so much sinking as colliding

with the jagged coast, the cliffs, like them
all floating up above the highest branches
of kelp they could have twisted into rope
to anchor them, something like the rafts

Aran Islanders made from strands of seaweed
to drift back inland with the tide. He tells
how they made it safe ashore at last, the hull
of the *James Caird* battered, worn thin

as an upturned mussel shell, or maybe
leaves them there, still hanging on somehow
above the kelp, suspended in mid-air.

Previously published in *Coast to Coast to Coast*, 2018

Footnotes to a river
By Cindy Botha

1. Pine trees are confirmation that darkness clings erratically. The river-gums, on the other hand, are pale as thighs.
2. A streambed knuckled with pebbles.
3. In conversation with the river, you will not match its fluency.
4. Bellbird, stitchbird, waxeye, plover, swallow. The gas-blue flare of a single kingfisher.
5. A waterfall is water ¦ rock ¦ air in exactly equal parts.
6. Here, dogs emerge dripping from their peaty plash and wallow, mouths open as lilies.
7. From the thickets, cicada static.
8. Stare at the surface until your eyes overflow with dazzle, and a thousand small fish look back at you.
9. By midday, the river is polished greenstone.
10. (i) Longfin eels loiter in the backwater.
    (ii) Chicken livers make good eel bait. But if you lie on the bank in the warm afternoon and watch, you might leave empty-handed, your head full of ripple and quiver.
11. Emerald dragonflies feast on a rabble of gnats.
12. Bullrush, flax, floating fern, ribbonwood, swamp-grass, mangrove, sedge.
13. The river will outrun you, always.
14. A half-drowned bee will climb to the tip of your thumb, shiver the wet from its wings.
15. In 2006, an unprecedented spate took the footbridge. All night it boomed through dreams, chilled pillows with spray.
16. Shrugging off branches, the moon reminds pooled elvers of their path to the sea.
17. Night drops from the trees, adds its dark tassels to the river.

Previously published in the *Ink Sweat & Tears* webzine by IS&T Publishing,11/03/2022

Every time I think of rain, it's you
By Claire Booker

apocalyptic,
tympanic on bins,
drenched beyond dreich, gone
before you arrive, on the slant, tensile,
colour of bitumen, biting, spitting, driving, a wind-herded
squall drunk on isobars, smell like green thunder,
like a car crash, like a direct hit, a flick in the eye, prismatic,
on the wrong side of the court,
seeping like a commitment, like a withholding, like the pearly nap
of a lawn, sheets of you, flush as furrows, a lip-smacked pond O< O< O
skinny dipping in my pools straight from the hip,
barbelled as a cat fish, sun-prickled,
crop-wrecking, slick
on the tongue,
feather-light, falling
in nano
drops
drip, drip

drip

drip

Waiting for Cranes
By Clara McLean

You'll sit and watch for hours,
days, before you see them.
You've been known to turn

to oracles to help you read the sky,
like Jean, a docent at the Sacramento
preserve, who's set up tripods

on its mud divides, and promises
the sandhill cranes will come by sunset,
though she can't say

where. You've walked all day
around the delta, plumbing its archival
depths, through places

where Chinese laborers lived
separately, working
the agricultural miracle, in wooden towns

they built but weren't allowed to own.
Years of stooping waist-deep
in the wetland in the heat

moving mud for levees to turn flood plains
into plenty. In the old saloon, displayed
above a dusty abacus:

a painting of two cranes,
arched necks encircling
the ideographs for luck.

Some folks believed
the cranes were harbingers
of fortune, their huge flocks

reinventing hope
as the valley slowly wrung out
into fruit trees, rice, asparagus,

the native oaks parched
and probing downward. Some
turn or wish has led you

to this point--alone
on a park bench,
waiting. You squint

into the rusting sun, at trees
shabby from years of drought,
reclaimed ponds boiling with tadpoles.

At last, a thin scree in the distance.
They pop through the near dark:
the cranes float in by hundreds

as you watch each bird turn flame—
slim wick swiped by red
and bottomed by a burst

of brightness--flicker
of the day that's gone,
light for those approaching.

River
By Corinne Casella

I envy the water its movement
It never questions, it simply flows
Though rocks and falling leaves
may divert its course for a time
its faith never waivers
Secure in the surrender
that the path is the destination

The Muddy Chicago Portage
By Cynthia Gallaher

Illini Indians spotted
two in a canoe,
plus their crew,

French-Canadians
Louis Joliet
and Pere Marquette,

Vying their way
up the Mississippi River
back to the Great Lakes.

The route you want to take,
said the Indians,
is a mistake,

There's an easier,
watery route,
with a little portage in between.

So, in their voyager canoe
of birchbark, lashed in spruce,
with seams sealed in pitch,

They headed
diagonally
off the Mississip.

Up the Illinois River and Chicago River,
connecting to the Des Plaines,
they portaged their crafts

Around marshy Mud Lake,
just north of today's
Midway Airport.

To an area called Checagou,*
via a small river**
to the mouth of Lake Michigan.

Joliet and Marquette were there, the first
non-Indian pair, to cross
the muddy Chicago portage, in that year 1673.

Who would never see 200 years later,
Chicago become the busiest port
in the U.S,***

On that huge
inland sea,
where our city's pressed.

*Checagou – land of the stinking onion, ie. Chicago
** This small river was the south branch of the Chicago River
***By 1882, Chicago became the busiest port in the U.S., attracting more ships
 annually than New York, New Orleans and San Francisco combined.

Water
By D.A.Prince

runs in the family, my father says
plumbing the rough hedge, deep
in hawthorn, bramble, till his hands
recognise the fit of hazel. One slice
with the knife I'm never allowed to touch
and it's sprung, his trap
for mapping springs and their secret
underground channellings.

He picked it up,
its twisted fluent tongue,
easy as speech, his father's trade.
Born to bricks, he took for granted
native bonds, their strength in walls or wells,
and skills like mixing mortar, levelling,
and sealing off; and likewise
how the hazel dipped and reared
compelled by liquid signals,
codes of water translated
down Plynlimon's torrents and sour rushes,
slipping into thin soil through shale.
Perhaps the day he learned was like today:
late May, young lambs now clever with grass,
blackbirds as sharp as slate
scoring their songs on the blue air.

Walking this stubborn field,
stumbling, my hands closed within his, pulse to pulse,
I feel the hazel buck and curve, watch
in wonder the wrenching message as it tracks
the clean lie of water.

Published in *Nearly the Happy Hour*, Happen*Stance* Press, 2008

Cryptid (The Mystery of Water)
By Daniel Hinds

'the water cascading and churning like a simmering cauldron'
– Robert Campbell, 'Strange Spectacle on Loch Ness', Inverness Courier, 1933

Let me decipher your key.

The neck that curves like the line of beauty
Of the poem I intend to write some-point tomorrow.

The slow wet grace of the snail skin shadow,
The liquid and unheard word of a gainsaid grail.

The water cascading and churning
Like a witch's shimmering cauldron.

The taste of loud slurped primordial soup.
And the smell of the afterburp.

The lock of uncut hair that gets in your face.
And the blur of your finger's quick flick.

A trick of black and white.

The high and demonic denomination
Of a cryptocurrency.

The password that is simply "uncrackable."

When we find the beast, snacking in its nest,
Roll the soft white of our eyes over its ruminant neck,
Drag it to shore and lock it to a shape,

We'll only ask it what weird white fish lives unblinking
Beneath its slime, and, unanswered, toss it back.

Previously published in *The Honest Ulsterman*, October 2020

Water
By David Thorndale

At dawn on New Year's Day my grandmother opened
her eyes, spoke her very last word, then left this world.
My brother thought she wanted a drink from the cup
on the bedside table she had been using for months.
My mother said her mind was reliving the memories
of washing Sunday dinner dishes in a bright kitchen.
My sister approached it all somewhat philosophically
with the idea of returning to the walls of the womb.
I saw her soul as a bird breaking free from the rocks:
the white tips of wings above the white tips of waves.
The four of us stood there bathed in glorious sunlight,
touched by a word we had never really heard until now.
It came and echoed like an answer from the other side,
like a divine truth spoken at the start of the New Year,
like a gift given for each of us to open in our own way.

Beach Music
By Derek R. Smith

That particular sloshy squish
Of a wet long-haired dog
Running, honoring its freedom
Pads gently pushing down on
And then gravitating above soggy sand.
The couple argue-agreeing
About whether they have been
To this beach before
Or if it was the other one....
That shore a bit south from here.
Beach sounds
Exist in places that are made for healing,
The permeated sand that holds you,
Though it's confusing how
It holds itself,
Against rough tides and currents
Hammering not-so-solid
Million tiny grains
Stacked inside the water table.
The ocean that
Reminds of time
And change that comes
In every second of weathering
a relentless environment.
The special greenish-blue chime
That only rings
When salt water tickles
The upper needles of a coastal fir tree.
The joyful screams of children
Let loose

And immediately reverting
To their inherent ocean wildness.
Gleefully
Breaking the rules
To the beach game
They are only now creating.
And the waves too,
Always the waves.

Lightness
By Diana Wiese

I take my body to the water

To the pool-
Head under the surface
Noises drowned
Just the ambient sound
Of my breath
A moving meditation

To the sea-
My weightless body
In cyan-blue saltwater
Swimming on top of
A wave, a mountain
Carrying me closer to the shore

I come out of the water
Refreshed, energized, strong
My body heavy again
Grounded by gravity
My mind calm and restored

Cursive
By DS Maolalai

the trees pop and sway
in an effervescent bubbling:
sunlight through a glass
cracking ice cubes.

it's september: swallows
and housemartins
cluster, thrown like leaves
against driftwood
in an eddying river-
side, along with crushed
beer cans – soda
cans and other debris.
in the mornings

I look at them
landing – the end
of endless swoop. all summer
the river has been abuzz
lively – fly nymphs
and birds looping
cursive pursuit. the blue
note of freedom as swing
through the city. a diagram
of step-by-step
formal tie knots.

I wish I was going to africa.
they add style
to late afternoons. sometimes
I stand on my balcony
for fifteen minutes
or thereabouts or more.

Riverside

after George Seurat's 'The Bathers at Asnières'

By E.E. Nobbs

There's a little red dog
perhaps the artist's afterthought
in the lower left corner –
she's in the sun, the day looks hot.
Let's call her Rilla.

Red like the rusty keel
of a beached, battered sailboat,
she's the size of a baby seal,
but no inclination for swimming
– watches from the shore,

safe by her companion.
On the grass she smells the river's
tidal life and sewage, hears hollers
and laughter from the boy –
the little red dog is easy to miss.

And I did miss her the first two times.
Now Rilla's all I see.

Wave Rider
By Easkey Britton

Born on a new moon,
An ghealach nua,
In the darkness
where beginnings take root.
Our Mother drew strength from the sea
For both of us.
Breathing it deep inside.

Heartbeat, breath, ebb and flow,
A constant loving and letting go.
Fluid flow-lines ever-forming,
Break open the shell of perception
The wave a mirror to what lies beneath.

Time felt through the body
The skin of the senses awaken,
Becoming part of its pure movement.
The veil between the seen and unseen thin.
Colours bleed into each other.

A lonely wildness stirs
Under storm-beaten skin.
Alive with the memory of a seabird
The hollows of the ocean cry out.

In the space between the waves
A net woven from solitude
Unravels.
Suspended
In the beautiful essence of isolation
A desire to go down into the depths within
awakens.

Through the fissures and the fractures
Be with it all.
Breathe into the belly.
Let go
What wants to die.
Let emerge
What wants to be born.

The Shoal
By Ed Ahern

The shoal sour dries in wind drifts
as the leavings of the ebb come into view.
Shell piles here, sand there, rimmed by
barnacle rocks and wet-rotting weed.

Gulls and terns pick at scattered
remnants of crab and fish,
and lift dying clams high enough
to drop them onto the rocks.

The water almost, almost stops,
a hovering quiver in the shoal's edges,
before the surge rewets the gasping buried
on its slithering way across the crest.

Men who ignore this ever-change
are trapped by it.
One or two boats a year aground,
one or two men a decade drowned.

Feeding and dying quicken with the flow,
little fish pushed across the shoal
toward waiting jaws,
birds swooping for the crippled.

Force of water rules the shoal,
which heaves its crests and shallows
to appease the ever-flowing god
who never looks back.

The water climbs man-high above the shoal,
And, stirred only by wind
fondles fish and weed and shell
until ebbing implacably into turmoil.

Previously published in *Plum Tree Tavern*, 2019

Bream Head
By Eithne Cullen

Bream Head, like the silvery fish
lying in clear, blue waters,
green with shrubs and ferns
and gravel pathway through the fields.

The day is noisy with the calls of seagulls
and the tuneful singing of the morning birds.
We pass cows, with black-brown polished hides
like ancient furniture and sideways eyes
that shyly gaze as we walk by.

Around a bend one cow rests beside
the concrete edge of a gun emplacement
from the war, the heifer smooth and sleek,
the bunker hard and grey.

There are so many colours in the sea
I struggle for more ways to say "blue"
where it's deepest, *navy* or *French* won't do;
sunlight glints on polished steel
where they have built the oil refinery.

Five Parts Water
By Elaine Morrison

    I

Water fills
every   distracted
thought.

Being in it,
being on it.
Being it.

Salt water.
Fresh water.
Brackish water.

I am
immersed

in it all.

    II

What is a spirit
if not energy –
manifest in
                surf,
a tremoring frond
of seaweed,
      a tossed
   weave
of fishing net?

III

Empirical brains
fathom
the science
of ocean currents,
of hydrological cycles,
of river catchments,
                        flows
    and floods.

Reach   beyond,
deeper –
        abandon
rationality
to the subliminal,
the emotional,
the naturalness
of
being.

Be trout to the
feathered lure,
sailors to the
selkies cry.

IV

Without water
I am lost
in a   landlocked   no-where.

Equilibrium ceases –
off kilter,
           tossed
in a wind   ravaged
storm of   anxiety
                  beyond the blue.

V

Let me
slip
on weed-wrapped
rocks,
wet
my feet
in coldest brine –
set
     me
         afloat.

Ammonite
By Eleanore Christine

I am fascinated by the fact
that more than half the human body
is made up of water, more than blood
or organs or muscle or sinew.

I am amazed at the torrent in our arteries
a tempest sitting on our tongue, kept at bay behind teeth
we are a hurricane caged within bone, our fragile flesh
the only thing holding back the squall
and one day it might burst
and we would pour, we would flood
we would be free.

I am in awe of the power swimming in our veins
a reminder of our ancient origins -
how before mankind, two-legged and upright
we were once single-celled, marine-dwelling protozoa
how we then traded gills for lungs and scales for skin
fins split into fingers, lengthening into limbs
to come creeping, crawling, struggling, surviving
out of our aquatic, amniotic world
and finally gasp for air on dry land.

And I think about how, when I am a withered old woman
pale and waning as the crescent moon in the dusk of life
perhaps I would like to be taken to the riverbank
laid to rest in a casket of cattails and reeds
let the mud cover me, swallow me
wrapped in a cocoon of silt and clay
slowly turned to stone over millennia.

Let the currents reclaim me
carry me out to sea
and take me home.

Antarctic Blues
By Emily Tee

glacial blue's the colour of deep penetrating cold, first
absorbed through your vision then that biting chill you
cannot forget – long before the snowflakes fall
the frigid air freezes any exposed patch of skin in
seconds. It's the sound of ice candling that I love -
a crinkle-tinkle, bell-like music from shards with
pillared crystal structures and the specific blueness Antarctica
has a monopoly on. As we sailed onward the ice colonnades and
archway appeared in front of our boat, like magic. And then
we began to wonder what might be through there - it
could be the entry to a yet undiscovered domain that breaks
down the barriers of reality, because in this place your
head can never trust your eyes, and much less so your heart.

*Note: this is a Golden Shovel poem based on the quotation "first you fall in love
with Antarctica, and then it breaks your heart" attributed to Kim Stanley.
In a Golden Shovel poem the last word of each line makes up the chosen phrase.*

Previously published in *The Ekphrastic Review*, 24 April 2022
as part of their *Caponigro* ekphrastic challenge.

Underwillow
By Emmaline O'Dowd

Underwillow's a cool house with thinning thatch
autumn's started to unravel. Outside
the sun, still strong and mellow, warms shallows
where, patterned like riverbed pebbles,
minnows hover in reflected blue
above the gravel. On the river's slow mirror
each shed willow-leaf's a yellow stitch
through two sheer fabrics, water and air
where trees, rocks, swans, myself, find doubles.
A place where clouds and reeds collide.

The Timing of the Lightning and the Thunder
By Erica Vanstone

A storm approaches, pulling in heat and
charged particles. But a fire needs
oxygen to grow, and as you retreat,
I cannot help but follow. Together, we
count the distance of each blow—the
timing of the lightning and the thunder.
I watch the sky grow dim as the birds
take cover. I am drawn to its power,
not away from it—I hover, not under
the blanket, but over it to look
at the darkness and count every hour.

Like so many, you follow the lightning,
the white-blue flash, the brightening
as it strikes the hot vapor of the clouds.
But I am here for the thunder, the unseen
gusts and everything under the visible.
I am here for the contents, the corners of
the rains, the creases—the water,
and all that it releases. I can only trust
your thunder is the echo of my own
lightning far away; the rumble of it brushes
my ear as we draw each other near
and for a moment, everything is aligning.

Yet, I know, still, we count the timing
between the lightning and the thunder,
measuring the seconds between the
clashes; a monsoon that dashes away
the feeling that we could be something,
anything, other than what we are. A storm
is still a storm, whether hours or days.
It's not the urgency that matters, the
speed, but how far away the lightning
strays from the thunder. Only the distance
reveals what is meant to be outrun:
escaping the flow to rejoin the sun.

When I visit the river
By Eva Lynch-Comer

I crunch the spines of leaves
between my teeth and drink river water
seasoned with the leaves' sun baked bodies

fold flower petals in on themselves
to observe how they hold
those creases in their bellies

pour beads of water onto my wrist
create a bracelet of translucent pearls
skip on lily pads so my toes can sip the river

rub rose water on my ribs
cough old air out of my lungs
catch sun rays with my tongue

Previously published in *Yugen* by *The MockingOwl Roost*, December 15,2022.

Swimming at The Stockman Bar
By Francesca Leader

The signs on the windowless plywood wall
said "Coors," "Dance," and "Pool."
"Pool" was the one that tantalized—
Though Mother denied it, I couldn't believe
there wasn't something magical in that bar;
that those loop-gaited men
in dirty cowboy hats
and dirtier baseball caps,
all with feet that seemed half broken
(as if in the process of becoming fins)
weren't on their way
to a crystal-blue tank
around which they would shuck off the filth
of unwashed plaids and Levi's
to become leathery fish,
diving into the icy blue drink,
swimming

all the way to Alaska.

Previously published in *Stoneboat Literary Journal*, May 2022

In Your Mouth
By Freya Mavor

I think this would sound better in your mouth.
In your mouth you could sink a million ships.
Soaked in saliva linguistics; I don't speak
your language in all its riddles and tricks.
The weather warned you wanted me drowned
but I stuck around, a stubborn mariner.
The feeling of sinking the most profound nectar;
pulling me in and dragging me under - I became
an etymologist obsessed with your Siren Song,
gathering losses as one gathers stones
on a beach. I waited for waves to take me –
a creature lost at sea - to safety.
The chance to be buoyant, just once.

It takes time to translate love when it's violent.
To differentiate a rip-tide from a current.
To remember the tang, pure mess of your tongue
and not sink again, lament and be drowned.

Summer '22
By Gill Learner

I dreamed of rain, woke hoping to hear car tyres
shooshing down the road. I despaired
at TV updates: the fissured mud of reservoirs;
queues for bottled water; shrivelled crops;
farmers forking winter silage to their cows.

Ignored, the lawn turned to dustbowl beige.
I saved water from rinsing fruit and washing up
to pour round beans, tomatoes and courgettes;
refilled the birdbath; lamented roses
bending faded heads in prayer.

I sat through sporting news: arms slicing
turquoise water; the bounce and jump,
the precision twisting, folding falls through space
to shatter sapphire glass to silver spray; I yearned
to feel that silky coolness on my skin.

At last the weather changed: teasing showers,
sudden cloudbursts, then retreats. Chance
dictated where they fell – in places so fierce
the earth could not receive the rush so that it surged
into streets, under doors, down cellar steps.

But it was not enough. Never enough
to quench our burning world.

School Leaver
By Helen Evans

I spent that summer pigeonholing cheques
into alphanumerical order
behind the cramped machine-room's half-closed blinds,
fleeing at five to clock up thirty lengths,
each nine breast-strokes long, my goggled face
gulping in gobbets of air above water,
snorting out lustre-walled bubbles below,
again, and again, until I somehow stopped

pushing forwards - swam as though suspended
in the gap between one moment and the next,
hauling the pool's far blue edge towards me
with each heave of my arms, sensing the earth's
curvature scroll past on either side, then
watching myself from above, streamlined and flowing.

Previously published in *Space at the Table*, Hooper Publishing, 2011

Fenland Field
By Ian Clarke

Where pike and chub were gaffed,
where swallowtail butterflies
hid in the shimmering distance.

There were waves and jetties,
a splash of blue-grey sea
drained to a shiver,

where they ploughed up
a silver censer, an incense boat,
now a forest of wind-turbines cutting their teeth

against a frost sharpened moon.
I can still see him singling turnips, docking beet,
hands earthed in ice

and where I stop and watch, a ghost grey breeze
flits a quarrel of sparrows,
out where water comes up blind,

widens to lapwing, curlew and snipe,
leaving absence intact,
enough stars to freeze a path home.

Previously published in *Spelt Magazine* Winter, 2022/3

The Onsen
By Jade Brooke-Langham

I felt the fabric of the universe once in
rural Japan with a dear friend, completely naked,
steeped in the deliciously hot waters of a natural
outdoor onsen. It was dusk and I remember looking
up at the transitioning sky, through the frame
of a crooked wisteria wound above our heads.

The first stars stitched onto blue ombré, the sweet
scent of the overhead blooms skipped like children
to my inhalations, and the gentle cadence of my friend
conversing in Japanese nearby, enveloped me in a blanket
of sensation to be felt once and once only.

Audrey Channels a Love Letter
By James Gering

Dear Kherson, fertilising my heart even as
the bombs convert you to rubble, and the glee
of our children on the merry-go-round turns to terror.

I yearn for your soft glowing street lights
and the aroma from the cheese factory. I yearn for
what cannot be recovered: the lives of our loved ones.

My dear city, how we are changed.
Your people scavenge for safety and scraps
of dignity. They find shelter in cellars of sadness.

Remember Eva from the theatre who used to
feed the pigeons on your steps? A Russian bullet
ended her husband's life. She is having the baby alone.

Maria and Yuri are now devout drinkers. Carol alters
clothing for soldiers, from two limbs to one.
And Eugene has taken to swimming in your lake –

long distances of stroking and forgetting.
He will discover a Kremlin rocket in the lake's bank,
fins and backside jutting out for all the world to see.

Water
By Jane Hanson

The waves rose high
Our rusty broken boat
Sucked and tossed by the swell and dip of the sea
The waves rose high
An impenetrable wall
The sides of the tanker were in sight
Then hidden from view
The waves rose high
Voices whipped by the wind
Shouts robbed from mouths
Screams and cries unheard
The waves rose high
I looked down on myself
From a safe place
Out of this hell
The waves rose high
One man threatens to throw another man overboard
Throw your phones away
Jetison your past —fear for the future
The waves rose high
A thousand distress calls
Come help us
Come save us
The waves rose high
Arguments and howling
Tossed like a ball back and forth
Who is responsable in French or British
Coastal waters?'
The waves rose high
A mother and child amidst many men
Clinging to the wooden planks
Sickness and thirst
Churning inside and out
The waves rose high
Souls on this journey who had never seen the sea
And neither knew how to swim or survive in its depths

The waves rose high
A light appeared and blinded our eyes
A rope was thrown aboard
Clammering and desperate to escape
Hands clawed and grasped this lifeline
The waves rose high
The boat unbalanced
We were shunted to one side
Falling onto eachother
Limbs twisted and flailing
The waves rose high
The mighty dark sea opened her arms
To welcome this desperate crew
Into the icy water
And down, down, down.

Greed
By Jay Gandhi

As the heavens pour,
I set my eyes on the puddle.
New-born ripples come into form,
expand, grow, try to prosper.

Slowly the neonate expands its radius,
until impeded by siblings.
A fight starts for supremacy.
Eventually all the ripples lose.

A Fireman in the Blitz, Manchester, 1940
By Jeff Gallagher

Looking heavenward he saw devils
picked out by a floodlight's sabre
among the smoke and flame of the infernal sky.

Temporal monuments to the Lord
crumbled like Babel or Gomorrah
as the fire's acolytes raised their jets on high.

Blind Samson rent stones asunder
as prayers came from the buried
who hoped for heaven yet did not wish to die.

But this spire stood impervious
pointing its defiant finger
at each shrieking incendiary's satanic cry.

And the man who would be my father
formed a cross with his neighbour,
melted iron with water, and felt his spirit fly.

Van Gogh Revisits His First Painting as a Ghost
By Jenna K Funkhouser

I've seen this street hundreds
of times, sometimes
even in my dreams.

So what is it about one man,
slouching down the canal,
the light like dawn,
the way the lines
are stone and river
skeleton and key?

Fog makes us intimate,
shapeless, he and I
just a handful of neighborhood
undistracted by a wide expanse
of sky.

When the curtains part halfway
like a careless mouth
we flow like water
into their open lives.

Previously published in *Ekphrastic Review*, August 2023

Capel Celyn
By Jenni Wyn Hyatt

Last summer
the bones of my village,
long submerged,
emerged from reservoir mud.
No phoenix from the ashes, this,
just unimaginable sadness,
for a community dispersed,
a way of life lost.

I was just a girl
when we were forced from the valley.
An old woman now,
I've seen floods and gales,
heatwaves and droughts
but not on this scale.
Humankind was slow to concede
what was happening at first
but now self-interest and greed
will bleed the earth dry.

Capel Celyn was the Welsh village which was drowned to provide water for Liverpool.

Are Tears Tested for PFOA?
By Jennifer Chante

When I cry I cry the sea

saline   spill

back to lakes back to saltings

back to clouds tears rivering

back   to   rain

and to the pipes again.

Refugium
By Jeri Lewis Edwards

I am not
the confluence of spine, the flush-flash-
bash of a river's untethered soul,
the Verde, venerate falls in the Firehole, or fill of air
in lost smells... I am not
the Watersmeet, the place where our lips met,
those inconsequential discoveries. . . not
the Rappahannock, the rivulet not yet formed
in miscarriage, Bagaduce, Housatonic,
the cataract of rapids to your heart,
the crutch in the Snake, or the sinuous meanders from
the Columbia, the cliff
house set on a failed marriage,
where what we found by water's edge vanished
outside of dreams . . .
not the oxbow's abandoned loop of river channel
no longer recognizable in the wildness of our past,
or the Neversink, the receding San Pedro, nor
the surge of sea to the imperturbable estuary --
Instead, I'll be that vast migration, that
long-distance warbler, the Chiricahua Sky Island
where they'll carry my body in a burlap bag
to the 9,000-foot crest, lie me on sprigs
of Winterfat, fragrant Algerita, and leave me at last,
to the eternal song of the Hermit Thrush.

The Standardization of Raindrops
By John Lanyon

On emergence from the cloud
all raindrops will be assessed for symmetry
non-standard drops will be returned
for a fresh start
raindrops which linger
taking in the view
will be accelerated
less than transparent raindrops
will be polished before release
lonely raindrops will be integrated
freezing raindrops will be warmed
to a minimum of 5 degrees centigrade
raindrops with excessive, show-off surface tension
will be counselled
raindrops will not slide down window panes
raindrops will be proud of their patch of sky
failing clouds will be re-named
raindrops congregating in rainbows
will be dispersed
raindrops from nimbostratus clouds
will be viewed with suspicion.

No more puddles
no more splashing
no more reflections

Previously published in *Words Go Out to Play*, The Charlbury Press, 2018

Vespucci in a moment of lonesome clarity
By John Tessitore

The pace has slowed a bit
although no one likes to admit it.

After a period of furious activity,
hard labor, sweat, adrenaline,
creative energy,
the doldrums again.

We're all just wading, catching our breath
before the next big wave comes crashing.

Afraid to tread too long
or worse, afraid of sinking,
we kick up tiny splashes
and try to speed the tides,

but it's never enough
to bring us to shore,
and it's never the same ride.

And as we float along we're aging,
believing our minds are as young
and full of the same potential
as before the lull,
and that the past is ever-present,
as if nothing could ever be different
and every fact is fixed for our returning.

Patience.

Soon we'll skip across the surface again.
Too much self-reflection spoils the water
for everyone. Soon.

And yet...it comes anyway.

Even Poseidon himself cannot quiet
or still the restless, not completely,
and my anxious mind lists.

I'd always believed that I had problems
for which there were solutions,
depending on the voyage I chose.

Now, in the calm before the next surge,
in a moment of lonesome clarity,
I realize that I have issues

from which I will find no refuge.

North Fork, Flathead River
By Judith Mikesch-McKenzie

Sitting in his study, the poet told me that if there was a place
   where people did not live beside a river, he did not want
    to know it, or ever to go there.

I left his home and paced the seven-mile path along the Irish
   riverfront where both my grandfather and his
    once worked, and thought of

my father, thigh-deep in the North Fork, the mountains rising
   all around us, he casting his line over and over into
    the air, a shining lasso of spun silver,

flying through dazzling air, until the weight of bait and hook
   draws it down into the cascading waters.

Around the bend my mother stands thigh-deep in river cold
   as well, her red dress floating like a bride's train
    all around her as she,

one handful at a time, flings river-water into the air and lifts
   her laughing face to take it in as droplets fall.

I have known the spirits of the river, alive in the shallows,
   sparkling with sunlight, visible when the smell
   of rushing water swells in nostrils hungry
    for the flavor of liquid speed.

Everything in me moves with those sprites, flying close above
   them, near enough to reach down to the tumbling water
   and feel its reassuring bite.

I am the river's second, its apprentice and aide as it weaves around,
    sliding across the ground between the hills,
    sculpting and shaping, sometimes
    a deep waterway that men
    with ships can work,

and elsewhere running clear in the shallows, where lines of
    silver flash through the air, and young faces revel
    in the joy of falling water

unaware that, far away, near another river, a poet sits in his rooms
    and writes of the work his grandfather did,
    shoulder to shoulder with mine.

Weeping Woman
By Karen E Fraser

I fill the bath, pour into it
fragrant rose oil and a coconut bath-bomb
that quickly fizzles, forming liquid clouds.
I light a candle, two wicks bright,
steam challenging each flickering flame
to burn. I switch off the light and welcome
the enclosure gifted by shadows. Hung
from the ceiling above is a Weeping Woman
mobile, her weird abstraction swirls in the heat –

one large, powder-blue tear
strung beneath the thick, black
lashes of an oversized amber eye,
a raised brown eyebrow floating
beside a pointed pink nose
circling red, red lips –

beading sweat trickles down the nape of my neck,
tracking a path between my breasts, each drop
disappearing into the scalding, milky water
lapping around my dumpling-soft belly. In the quiet
I imagine trading the salty moisture in my cells,
the sensual, silky-sweet slipperiness inside me,
for all the rain that had to fall to fill this world with life.
Time blows out blissfully. I breathe deeply, dripping generously,
dissolving into the bath water until completely emptied.
I pull the plug and pour toward the ocean,
the silent depths of me returned
to the only place I have ever belonged.

The Shipping Forecast
By Kate Winter

My darling insomniacs, you have made it to 00.48

Viking North Utsire South Utsire

Our father Vikings are silent, but the sea roars in our heads and calls us back through
scandi noir, the love of bleakness and no-hopers, the first underdogs cowering in their
mud against blades
and muscles, those terrible Europeans -
our primal fears never leave us so now we have left them

cosying up with their fika, chocolate chaud, kannelbunnen, croissant, lebkuchen. Who
would want to give up all this? only the British mongrel sea-dogs, biting their own tails
not to mention the hands that feed them,
they are still circling, snarling, a shit show as they say.
Slap their bums and send them home. It's more than they deserve.

Forties Cromarty Forth Tyne

My blessed land of the flat language I have never seen you so angry, not since
the iron lady stole our hearts and buried them in the dark
can you remember that? Ask yer dad, mam, little one, you're too young to be
so dirty, covered in remnants, revenants, life's ashes taken from our own soil.
I think tomorrow we will see flags on the horizon and you will come and grace us.

Dogger Fisher German Bight
Humber Thames Dover Wight

So many songs. Our souls
follow the sirens and here they are, salted and raw
beached, sunk, drowned, shot or shut
into blank black nothingness as if the sea had taken them but it wasn't the sea it was
you, shouting no mercy you have forgotten how to sing you have forgotten the feel of grass
on your naked feet how the sun is, where you began

Portland Plymouth Biscay Trafalgar FitzRoy

Angel Fitzroy, I cry for you, but I miss the sinister sound of Finisterre -
the end of the earth. Are we there yet? I wonder how many times you asked this.

Did you think you had reached it, with the changes wrought had you done enough to doom us
But wonder is not a sin.

Are you weeping for me now?

Sole Lundy Fastnet Irish Sea Shannon Rockall
Malin Hebrides Bailey Fair Isle Faeroes Southeast Iceland

Other lands of my mothers fathers mothers, coming with nothing but hope.

Running Upwards
By Katherine Breeden

foreign waves migrate me   to natal streams

I follow its smell   out of the gravel   where I was a small fry

the pebbles tell me

       no woman would ever want to give more

cold coastal waters push me   to the mouth of the estuary

I've stopped   eating   fat, muscles, organs
I use my pink   running   upwards, rapids, falls, bear claws, hooks.

the pebbles tell me   I was born
here   I will die too

redd, my magnum opus   spawn   swimming
on my side   I turn my tail   so they can smell,
the smell of our stream

the pebbles tell me   that's the worst of it, and I

say

the worst is letting go

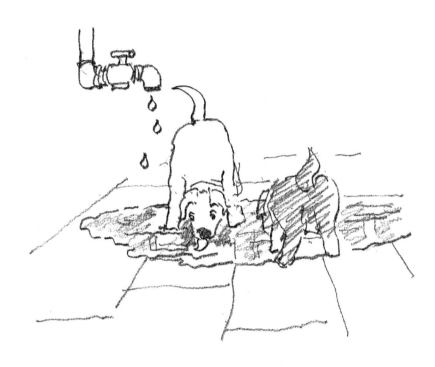

Untitled
By Katherine E Winnick

puddles forming
a stranded jellyfish
waits to return home

ritual:
By Katie Joyce Holmes

Prepare the bag, togs and towel,
Walking hymn is - just get in
Choose an alcove to perch between the regulars,
The silvers, the whites and the odd blonde out
Brisk and scurry to undress,
no time to

Stop,
keep going,

Feet first and then that bliss –
As up to your neck, this place begins.
At times, it is blue,
Today, it is sputtering,
November.
You won't stay long
A length or two, a piece of the sea.
We come down to claim it here
Out of our minds
Frozen, rushing and soundless
Blood and muscle
As you out,
Re-robe,
Usually, deliriously, talking to yourself
Out Loud, and strange, as we all are

Minute
By Kelli Weldon

I say I need a minute
when really I need weeks
to stay still,
let cold waves wash over my skin, make me
a seashell whorled and
strong, curved by the ages that have passed
sand whittling me into something clean,
something by the ocean that lies
in the sun alone and burns.

Somewhere in That Far-off Summer Land
By Ken LéMarchand

"A metaphysician in the dark, twanging
An instrument, twanging a wiry string..."
—*Wallace Stevens*

Look how they're strung   one by one
they fall to the grace of lissom fingers   plucked
blossoms set against winter's face   as if
their voices were stalwart locusts   among the reeds.

Nettled notes nestled nearest the bosom   where
froths an orotund hum upon   the water's edge;
fellow cottonwood's sea-green tongue   sung
lamentations under an undulating sun   in death.

There's no funeral for the—unstrung,
only the blue vervain of wild horses
      fading to white.

One by one, plucked, as if among the reeds
      where the water's edge sung in death
—unstrung.

Why carry sea glass
By Kristina Diprose

because
you wish you
could have stayed
on that wave-tossed
frosted beach
at Waternish,
the vast Atlantic
within your grasp
and because
you never
truly
believed
in sea eagles
until one soared
into solid fact
just as you
arrived
and because
you saw it as a
sign you were still
alive, mostly water
but still, and so broken
and wave-tossed
and frosted
but solid
as a jewel;
you knuckled it
into your pocket,
the alabaster sand,
the vast Atlantic,
the mythical
bird-like
being,
the salt
on your lips,
and now yearn
to be carried by tide
or sky, away, away,
because you wish
you could have
stayed

Previously published in *Coasts & Waters Anthology*, Susan Emmison, 2021

In Venice
By Lawrence Wilson

look: this window: arched and shadowed
that canal: narrow, deserted, secret
noonday sunlight turns its high-tide water to turquoise
a tiny church encrusted with coloured marble
a facade dripping with white statues of forgotten saints
families enjoying the obligatory gondola ride
(and one teenager always sullen-faced
resisting the allure of this sea-bound city)

after sunset, the wind changed
started blowing off the Lagoon
cooler, moist, scented with salt
I feel Venice change on my skin
I feel my skin change because Venice wants—
      something else?
      something more?
      some different way of seeing, waiting, wondering?

look: this window, lit after sunset
(ochre walls, a carved ceiling, a crystal chandelier)
look: that canal, one dim streetlamp halfway along
(promising wonder, danger
endless depths of time like water, like memory)

      a cat curves like a half-wild comma
      stops, stares
      vanishes, shadow into shadow
      and from the tiny square ahead, a burst of laughter

there will be more laughter
there will be more wine
there will be more time, deep as water

Pacific Chorus
By Lesley-Anne Evans

June hangs humid, and Spring Peepers
call their lungs out, beyond
the pasture fence. They are a wall
of sound, a wave of mud dwellers
all spit and polish in a lovestruck serenade
around the neighbour's pond.

Pacific Chorus of a thousand
perfect pitch, and all for a lithe
young thing in a hot chase
of the more and less suited.
She's empty bellied and he
is considering riparian delight.

She waits at the meadow's edge
while the all-male choir vies for her
and her sisters. The moon ball suspends time
in a woodland of knowing eyes. Skunk cabbage
unfolds herself, and the pond is abuzz
with fairy moth, mayfly, and water strider.

A green question lingers
like an eighth note on the stave
of her skin - his *dolce, delicato,
dolchissimo.* This is how he sings
to her, and this is how her cool flesh
will rise to meet him.

Portrait of James Brindley, Canal Engineer

After the painting by Francis Parsons, National Portrait Museum

By Linda Goulden

My stature's clear — in water, iron, stone.
Land's contours bend to my persuasion
as I ensure, without recourse to calculation,
two tunnel ends will meet as one.

Yet, to suspend creditors in hope
and channel new investment's eager flow,
this draughtsman's paid to survey me
and I to ape the drape of false nobility.

Fixed in this pose I ache for use,
my mind's eye spying all I do not do.
I labour here, to hold myself un-moved,
harder than labourers in navigation.

Physician, agent, wife and friends declare
good health a treasure to be sourced in rest.
I'll stand an hour — no more. What wealth
can be extracted from a pit of idleness?

Unstopped, I'll exercise my will
to draw my outline here in clay,
until my puddle's cracked
and life's force leaked away.

When slowing, close to dock,
breath narrows and limbs lock.
Then may my tired old bones
give thanks for their unloading.

Previously published in an edition of the canal magazine, *'One Seven Four'*.

I Am Beck
By Linda Saunders

Mistake me not
           for brook
some Alice-jump
               between lush shires
no simpering streamlet me
no purling rill in a cushy bed

quicker   wilder
           beck I be
                becoming
river any moment –
             trickle to torrent
in a hectic dash from
           my fell parent
who makes the storm with his frown
and passes it on
        to his offspring

Secretive   truculent
             rocks in my throat
eels in my gut
        I can flash-flood   spate
drown a sheep
        wreak havoc –

following lullaby weeks of dazzle and dawdle
below milky ways of water crowsfoot
shade of alder and the lean-low hazel

with playpools for trout
             shelves and narrows
where they idle
     or lurk
       in a slick of shadow
practice polish and vanish
in the camouflage speckle I taught them –

beck at my best
       idyll reflecting
            dragonfly flicker
swallow-skim   daydreams poised beak of heron

The Lovely Stones
By Lisa Low

Many lifetimes of ocean waves have
washed their outermost surfaces away,
deriving them by slow degrees from
a single massive rock: egglike or oblong;
striped or stippled; green or speckled gray.
Unlike these Connecticut barnacle
pebbles pocking my gravel drive, these
lovely Nova Scotian stones, carried from
shore to shore clandestine in my car,
comfort me not only by beauty, but
by promise of eternity. Though even
these sea-razored rocks will not last. Holding
these talismans of still-stored sun in my
hands, how endlessly cold the stars tonight.

Swell
By Madeleine S. Cargile

And maybe the rushing in my veins isn't blood but a monsoon
The roaring tides that shattered the ships of greed-ridden sailors
Seeking to tame waters that were never meant to be domesticated
My rage is a storm held back by paint-slathered skin
That stretches and writhes with each curtailed comment
Every forced smile and waved hand
The hurricane flexes as I grip the armrest
And rise from my chair

The Queen of Scotland's Eleven Month Winter

after Castle Island and Cracking Ice, Patricia Macdonald

By Maggie Mackay

Crack a patch of ice, look down to the image:
Mary's cracking heart, her redhead fire smothered

by enclosure, poison, miscarriage of twins,
her host turned jailor, iced coating of mannerliness.

The tower house of stone, its cold air, imprisons her pain,
such icy chambers, northern winds bringing trouble and strife.

Forced out by her cousin, her spirit, an icy sadness,
haunts the air, seeking the company of her babes.

A Sea of Drowned Sailors
By Marc Brimble

The noise
could be the ocean
a tide
retreating
leaving stars
maybe I will steal a boat
drift away
among
whales
sharks
octopus
drowned sailors.

The Gap the Poet Left is Full of Water
By Margaret Beston

The men who own the rain fill the valley
with run-off from the hills, divert the Elan
from its seaward course, lay a pipeline
to bring fresh water to a disease-ridden city.

They reshape the landscape: trees swept
away, choked by rising flood, are replaced
with groves of larch and fir. The drowned church
is rebuilt – a romantic feature on the horizon.

Aqueducts stretch elegant limbs over tracks
and streams. Navvies quarry local stone,
construct dams of monumental grandeur
adorned with gothic towers and parapets.

Picturesque cascades thunder down
into Caban Coch where crushed walls
of Nantgwyllt – the house Shelley loved –
stare blankly upwards.

When the Elan Valley reservoir, Powys, was built in 1894, a house where Percy Bysshe Shelley once lived was submerged. He himself drowned at Lerici, Italy, 8 July 1822.

Dancing Fountain
By Marianne Brems

Random renditions,
of complex water jets,
height,
duration,
erupt in
symphonic patterns,
from a street level fountain
into the penetrating heat
of the town square.

Smiling children taken
by unpredictable rhythms
of ever changing streams
rush through a gap
in the broken curtain of water,
shoulders drawn,
arms lifted,
smiles dissolving into laughter--
Repeat, then repeat,
wet clothes pasted to skin.

Fewer more prudent adults,
beckoned
by the soul of the fountain,
plan their course
between the chords
of a liquid melody.
Gleefully they dart through
with measured precision,
just once, maybe twice,
helpless to outsmart the dance,
unwilling to soak themselves
before enchanted onlookers.

Unconcerned,
this intricate orchestra
continues bursting skyward.

Previously published in *Nightingale & Sparrow*, Issue 2 May 16, 2019

Blue Embrace
By Marie Papier

He wriggles his way
into the niche
where she hides

pulls her by the hem
of her pearly skirt
into his swirl

Her arms curl in lovelocks
unfurl around his body
in a tender hug

as he clasps her mantle
his jaw clenched
into her delicate flesh

She fondles his ear
slips a limb through
his open gill

deep   deeper still
suffocating
her lover's plea

His tail squirms
his body pleads for air
till he releases his prey

Gathering her frills
the octopus slides away
from his cold eye

Previously published in *Voices for the Silent*, an anthology for the
League Against Cruel Sports, Indigo Dreams Publishing, 2022

Water

for Conor

By Michael Farry

He waters our pot plants in the light rain, loves
the slap and dribble on geranium and fuchsia,
unconcerned with rotting roots or leaching nutrients.

When his watering can is empty he looks up,
asking me to turn the tap on, refill.
We laugh at the spillage, splash in the overflow.

If these survive the winter I'll take spring cuttings,
give him some of his own to care for,
replace them if an unexpected early frost kills them.

He'll not know the difference, unaware of the
quick turnover, how year by year I lose
perennials and vivid annuals flush and fade.

Someday, when water is more precious,
in a dry season, I hope he'll remember this,
how good our garden was, when it seemed

grandfathers could do everything.

Previously published in *The Age of Glass*, Revival Press, Limerick, 2017

Memory
By Michele Rule

Four-foot snowdrifts white
wind blows giant flakes through the air
I slip off my shoes and socks
undo my robe and dart
across the icy path
slipping silently into the pool
of water
So warm
Slight smell of sulphur
vapour rises lazily
and where the falling crystals
meet the steam
they transform, enchanted
Solid, gas, liquid
the magic of water

Untitled
By Michelle V. Alkerton

glistening
his sprinkler play
puddles on the floor

The Ripple of the Sea
By Mike Hoskin

The ripple of the sea
Is the only sound
As I watch the sun go down
It shines a red glow upon the sea
As it slowly meets the horizon
Seems to make a path for me

salt water pool by the ocean
By Mirjam Mahler

pool by the ocean
liquid meditation swim
morning waves salute

it's early morning
still not fully day
slip out of bed
tiptoe into the kitchen
quick espresso
hop on the bike
the sun barely awake
tinting the sky pink

pedal to the beach
eyes closed for a few seconds
inhaling the salty air
waves greet from afar

slip out of clothes
the worn out bathing suit
has inked a white tattoo
on my swimmer's back
bare feet skip
trying not to linger
on the cold ground

I nod to the two swimmers
going up and down the lanes
we never speak, respectfully honor
our quiet morning space

dip my toe, then climb in
a cold water greeting
its warm embrace rising up my skin
fumble with goggles
take a deep breath
dive into liquid meditation
accompanied by the sound
of the waves crashing
in the neighboring ocean

waves are not jealous
know that I will come and play
in the afternoon

About Hymn to Rivers
By Monica Kakkar

I have translated, The Hymn to Rivers, from the Sanskrit language, exclusively, for this anthology.

I recite this prayer in Sanskrit every time I pray, after lighting a ghee lamp. It is integral to my daily, weekly prayers, including auspicious days, festivals, fasts, monthly solar transits, solstices, equinoxes, eclipses, and especially to celebrate the birthdays of holy rivers.

Worshiping the five elements, through hymns, mantras, and mindful living, expressing gratitude, celebrating the interconnectedness, appreciating their presence around me, and within me, including all things in the Universe— is the core of my practice of Hinduism. Hinduism is a way of life ...

I have shared the glossary, and quick pronunciation guide, ahead of the hymn, to enhance your reading experience. Thank you.

Glossary:
Abode of Vishnu: Heaven

Nāradīya Purāṇa: Name of one of the many Purāṇas. The Purāṇa refers to Sanskrit literature preserving ancient India's vast cultural history, including historical legends, religious ceremonies, various arts and sciences, and date to at least several centuries Before the Common Era (BCE). https://www.wisdomlib.org/purana

Pronunciation:

Please follow the International Alphabet of Sanskrit Transliteration (IAST) at https://en.m.wikipedia.org/wiki/International_Alphabet_of_Sanskrit_Transliteration

Quick Pronunciation Guide:

rā: raa
ā: aa
vē: way
ē: ay
hī: he, me
ī: ee
Ś: Sh as in show
Śon: shown
mod: road
o: no, go, yo, flow, grow
yū: moo
ū: oo
Kau: Cow

Hymn to Rivers
By Monica Kakkar

I shall now recite the hymn to rivers which destroys all sins
Bhāgīrathī, Vāraṇāsī, Yamunā, and Sarasvatī

Phalgunī, Śoṇabhadrā, and Narmadā, Gaṇḍakī, and also
Maṇikarṇikā, Gomatī, Prayāgī, and again and again

Godāvarī, Sindhu river, Sarayūvarṇinī, and also
Kṛṣṇavēṇī, Bhīmarathī, Khāginī, Bhavanāśinī

Tuṅgabhadrā, Malharī, Varadā, and Kumudvatī
Kāvērī, Kapilā, Kuntī, Hēmāvatī, Haridvatī

Nētrāvatī, Vēdavatī, Sudyotī, Kanakāvatī
Tāmraparṇī, Bharadvājā, Śvetā, Rāmēśvarī, Kuśā

Mandarī, Tapatī, Kālī, Kālindī, Jāhnavī, and also
Kaumodakī, Kurukṣetrā, Govindā, Dwārakī, there are,

Brāhmī, Māheśvarī, Mātrā, Indrāṇī, Attrīṇī, and also
Nalinī, Nandinī, Sītā, Mālatī, and Malāpahā

Sambhūtā, Vaiṣṇavī, Vēṇī, Tripathā, Bhogavatī, and also
Kamaṇḍalu, Dhanuṣkoṭī, Tapinī, Gautamī, and also

Nāradī, and river Pūrṇā, all the rivers are named
One who recites daily, in the morning, especially when taking a bath

Destroys by remembrance, sins committed during millions of births
Attains happiness in this world, and goes to the abode of Vishnu.

Thus, the hymn to rivers in the Nāradīya Purāṇa is complete.

Woman Life Freedom
By Nasrin Parvaz

Shot, handcuffed to the flag rod.

He asked for water
the guards held a cup of water
out of reach and said, 'Take it.'

His mother came at dawn
with a bowl of water.
She was shot.

His sister came
with a bowl of water.
She was shot.

His cousin came
with a bowl of water.
She was shot.

His neighbour came
with a bowl of water.
She was shot.

His lover came at dusk
together with women.
Each holding a bowl of water.

Frightened
the guards ran away.

This poem was inspired by the killing of Khodanor Lajehie in this way by the
Islamic regime of Iran in 2022.

The Summer You Went Away to Washington
By Niall M Oliver

Every time I looked at the sky, it was as grey
as every picture of Abraham Lincoln I'd ever seen,
and the rain streamed incessantly down my window panes.

This isn't a metaphor to explain
how I was feeling without you—
it really did just piss down the whole summer,

and I felt like crying every day.

Untitled
By Noel King

the tide aways my footprint
remaining evidence
I was ever here

The Boat
By Oenone Thomas

The toy boat was made
of spare wood and painted
blue — this I remember.

I liked the colour blue
and you for setting me afloat.
The toy boat was made

and we took a bag of crusts
to the lake it was
blue — this I remember.

You, in colour block tank top
called me Ducks.
The toy boat was made

and I thought the crusts were for me.
Later, there was cake and I knew.
Blue — this I remember.

Told to wait at the lychgate,
I walked to the lake.
The toy boat was made
blue — this I remember.

The loch breathes
By Orla Beaton

Like an in-breath,
    the loch swelled,
it soaked the tree roots
    and sunk the pier,
it spread over the sands
    and filled the sluice gates.

Like an out-breath,
    we are left standing,
on sodden planks
    and insurance claims,
around mud-stained photos
    and broken hearts.

Like an inbreath,
    they came:
with offers of tea, warm fires
    and kindness,
with buckets, open arms
    and knowing human eyes.

Like an outbreath
    we face:
the uncertain unknown,
    we feel
the sorrow of dreams,
    we breathe in
the possibility of new ones.

Previously published in Orla´s 2nd booklet, *My Magpie Mind*, November 2022, and in her local community newsletter, *Kinross Newsletter*, April 2020.

City Sand
By Patricia Behrens

All the way home, Brooklyn
to Manhattan on the Q train,
I feel beach sand, a little gritty,

inside my shoes, under my toes,
real as the blasts of warm air when
the doors open for above-ground stops

before the subway cars go hurtling
underground with all of us—
city dwellers, urban strangers.

The sand begins to irritate, to maybe
start a blister, but I don't try to brush it off.
I like my secret reminder of nature,

of the sea close to city skyscrapers,
of the springy feel of beach sand, so hot
my feet almost burn, the feel of

cold currents, stronger near the jetties,
as I swim by the Aquarium (right by its
shark tank!), sighting by the Coney Island pier,

of catching glimpses with every breath of the old
Parachute Jump, the Wonder Wheel, the Cyclone,
of walking half-naked from water to boardwalk,

rinsing my feet under an outdoor spigot
but picking up sand again crossing the boardwalk
to put on street clothes for the subway, sand

stubbornly clinging to my feet through toweling,
all of this my secret as I sit here, a faint smell
of ocean still in my hair, sand clinging to my body

until I wash it off in the shower in Manhattan,
pleased with how it still tries to cling
to the tub and resists going down the drain.

shared depths
By Purnima Ruanglertbutr

just like the ocean
our lives whirl
in directions and depths
that only you alone
can experience -
yet, how comforting it is
to know that we are all swimming
in the same ocean
finding our way
through the waves

Untitled
By R.C. Thomas

the flow and
　　　　the ebb and
　　　　the duck of
the platypus

Previously published on *Heliosparrow*, 11/7/21 and *"Faunistics"*.

A Jigsaw Puzzle of an Adoptive Family
By Renee Cronley

When the clouds build inside him,
we go to the beach to break them up.
    I understand what it's like
to be born of a storm
to be made wreckage on the lonely island
of a developing young mind.
    I spent my life
putting myself together
so I could do it for another.

The waves roll in and reach for him—
I have to stop him from getting too close
and thwart the fluid manifestation
of all he feels but can't articulate
to keep him from drowning in them,
while leaving him enough space
so the progress we've made
doesn't wash away.

I pick up a conch shell
and hold it to his ear
    so that he could listen to
our amniotic beginnings.
The salt in our blood, like that of the sea,
    ties us together.
I melt into his smile
as he fits his small hand in mine—
    two unrelated pieces
from different puzzles
create a picturesque scene
of a family bonding along the seaside.

The spaces in between
By Rob Primhak

It's all to do with pressure
– osmotic or oncotic,
I can't remember which –
a boggy swelling of the tissues
as water in her veins
cannot be readily retained
but leaks out slow and steady
into the spaces in between.

By pressing gently and relentlessly
I leave my thumbprint in her little leg;
it stays – a potter's mark in clay.
Kwashiorkor, they call it
the advent of another child
and this one put aside
trying to stay alive
in the spaces in between

Resuscitation isn't simple
when a body's waterlogged,
veins imperceptible in swollen limbs.
I screw a squat thick needle
resolutely into her shinbone
deep inside her marrow
then squeeze in a fluid bolus
counterintuitively.

The place I should be starting is not here
at the wrong end of the journey
pushing my finger into a single hole
in a crumbling dam
as waters flow around me.
We're in a futile situation,
me and the swollen girl,
born or displaced into
the spaces in between.

Bass in the river
By Romina Ramos

You can see the bass in the river
a luminous slow dance in darkness
a handful of underwater flames.

You can hear it from the south pier
the ripples almost like a sonic pulse
beating to the breathing of the drums.

You can feel it if you sink your toes
where sweet water turns ocean face,
strings in the wind rave in the waves.

You can smell it across the bay
slick bodies floating above the shore
when it reaches us it's less pungent.

You can still taste it in the first sip
of morning tide, the sea salt washes
away the remains of the crowd.

The Memory of Water
By Sally St Clair

is it here
in the glass rings
dropped
by the trees
held
in the upturned
cups of ivy
in silvered holly leaves
reflecting
the sun

the elephant faced root
is lordly and watchful
the stream's
a piddling boy
fat pink hands
of rhubarb
thrust through
the cold and

the icicles are
a taste of smoke
they say water
has memory

I bring you a bucket of ocean from sea wall splashback at Robin Bay
By Sandra Noel

Dip each finger in turn. Feel the cling on your skin,
watch the water displace and crimpoline over.
Crab-walk your hand through the spadeful of sand.
Swish out the three hidden periwinkle shells
and uncover the silken-black pebble you gave me
thousands of high tides ago, swimming at Archi.
Float your palm up with the tendril of bladderwrack,
hear it whisper in the voice the sea breathes.

When you're shouldering the weight
of a cruise liner in dry dock,
I ask the sun to seek out your face,
the tingle of salt to fresh the air around your bed.
We conjure the shrill of gulls
and sway gently to the beat of being.

(Bays named are in Jersey.)

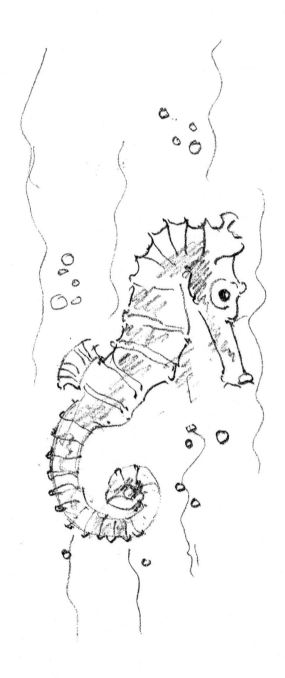

A Gander Speaks of Love
By Sarah Cain

Meet me on the field of gold, where sheep once grazed
But who now stand upon the rubble of dry stone walls
Meet me here and I will show you diamond encrusted waters
A place I will dance the courtship of love
In return for yours.

Meet me on this golden field, where winter is unusually kind
A place we can shelter in the gloaming, before waters call
Meet me here and we will lay our future in long grasses
A place we can shield for twenty-eight suns and moons
In return for familial love.

Meet me at this magical place, where our fledglings stand
Every new footstep their safe passage to shore
Meet me here and we will teach them a cacophony of sound
A song that encapsulates their heart
In return for ours.

Meet me here until feathers scatter over the dam
And shadows cast are yours and yours alone
Meet me here in the loneliness of your dreams
A place I will find you and pillage your grief
In return for loves goodbye.

small rituals

after Ada Limón

By Sarah Jeannine Gawthrop

i would make a ritual of willow branches kissing stony creeks
as i cradle you in my arms /as your mottled body / tender fur
rests in my cupped palms
as i pull you from the jowls of that austrian water cat
seemingly docile and unassuming / a purveyor of springtime carnage
your tiny heart slogs / struggles to pat
as my twelve-year-old / tear-stained / freckle-specked cheeks huff
discordant emotions on a sweet-smelling morning
so much death / especially this little lovey / this little bunny
how i buried you tenderly in a box by that creek bank
dirt in my fingernails / hatred for cats sewn into my heart
the circle of life is too much for this tender young mind
who thought she was coming to the english countryside
to drink tea /eat scones /visit castles / stroll in fields
if there's a lesson in this tender baby bunny death / i don't want it
give me sweeping stupidity and blissful ignorance
having your eyes opened is nature's cruellest trick
and yet / the duality of a beautiful death moment in spring –
is etched in my mind forever

Portmahomack
By Sarah Tait

Echoes of stillness
Hanging softly on evening's deepening peace
Calm as the slow beat of wings
Holding the flickering shadow
Steady on the water.
How easy tonight
To forget the weary tune of heavy fears
Lifted in the smoothing folds
Of quiet dusk; and the sun low and
Steady on the water.

River of India
By Shamik Banerjee

Whether the Narmada or Cauvery,
Which province has not your tributary?
You, mother of India- eternal and free;

For the mother who launders her saree,
For the dawn-bathing of the pujari,
You come for their ministration, unbrokenly;

The father for his child, comes at its birth,
And child for father when he leaves this earth,
And ash-beadaubed aghori, for his dip of mirth;

To yeomen and crops, you're the big wellspring,
To the fishermen, you great fordeal bring,
And to an atoner, his sanctum for purging;

Where'er you course, bear a new epithet,
Its grand endemic reverences get,
And in the denizens' hearts, culturally set;

Towards Arabia or Bengal's Bay,
An estuary does longingly stay,
For your fast arrival and mergence with its way;

Tennyson praised you in his Brook's water,
Poe described you through Alberto's daughter,
Your deific form pleased Shantanu and he sought her;

To a fretting mind, you're the pour of ease,
At times the truculent wrecker of peace,
Self-judge to largen your flow, self-judge to decrease;

You sustain faith in the ghat of Assi,
At Manikarnika, a sprite's mukti,
For ashes of mankind, the last sanctuary;

Whether from Shiva's braid or Nilgiri,
Whether Dravidian or Kashmiri,
You, mother of India- eternal and free.

Between the Waters
By Shane Coppage

The ocean is the sound of the color black.
The rhythm of absence.

The color black is the color of light.
The cadence of nothing.

Light is a mark of birth between the waters.
The ledge of dawn silver running.

A tight-rope trick about
the curve of the day as it

hews to the darkless night of the
urban forest and the great cobalt bulb

pressed up and against the
thumb-cut arc of the naked atmosphere.

Witnessed through the squares,
sagacious masses go by in waves as

Mother's scrim bottles the brutal gulf and her
brazen boss makes central its vaulted core.

Makes the color of the ocean the sound of black.
Absence, the color of light.

Green Turtle
By Sharon Larkin

Heavy lidded, she hauls bulk over clinker
to a meagre patch of sand on this volcanic
outcrop, to set her flippers digging.
They're better designed as propellers than spades,
inadequate blades for flicking silica, scooping
a dip for a clutch of soft-shelled ping pong balls.

She cries her midnight tears, drags her dome
to the spume, paddles her giant helmet back
to Brazil, to await her date to mate again, turn
turtle to this mid-Atlantic dot to do it all over.
Watch, meanwhile, for a twitch in the grit
as mini disks emerge from their depression

to zigzag seaward, if not picked off and scoffed
by frigate birds, trailing a carnage of sprogs,
a scatter of abandoned jamjar lids. But a few,
not upflipped by swooping bills, will scamper
to water. Hatchlings, out-manoeuvring marauders,
defying gulls, gullets and intestines – not sunk

to the benthos, but braving waves, their compass
set to the west, aiming for Fortaleza and Natal.
Daughters will go on breeding, as ill-advisedly,
barely making a dent in dipping rates of survival.
Back and forth in swell and foam they go, at risk
of crash of surf, dash against rock, gnash of beak

in the annual gamble of turtle sink or swim.

Previously published in *The Blue Nib*, 24 July 2020

Olive Tree in the Occupied Territories, Palestine
By Steve May

i suck in
the unfettered sun
i create deep shadows
with my dense canopy of leaves
three boys sit under me,
basking in a plastic pool
i know
water
the
simpli
city
of water

From a photograph in Tanya Habjouqa's Occupied Pleasures, winner of the World Press Photo Award 2014. The photos offer glimpses of day-to-day life across the occupied Palestinian Territories.

Geography
By Sue Burge

a world between my palms   shaggy outlines of many lands   no-one is speaking of water but this globe is dripping   what is the difference between sea and ocean   who marks the borders dictates when it slips from warm silk to cold stubble   does the North Sea speak with Anglo-Saxon vowels   does it say fuck when it forgets to turn the tide   does it read my tears dropping like braille and know the why of me   all this in my hands   spinning like a top pulled from the toe of a Christmas stocking   sometimes I prefer the slow motion of maps   if they all unfolded at once like tired origami birds I would drown in grids of squared and calculated blue   and I would go quietly   mouth closed   lungs trying to remember

Droplets
By Sue Spiers

What is the language of water
with no mouth, no larynx, no tongue?
Does water speak?

Does a stream sing?
Each note struck on rocks,
like a xylophone of stones.

Does a waterfall guffaw?
Transmitting the joke down,
fall about, laugh like a drain.

Does rain gossip?
Spread its tittle-tattle, spit spittle
at breeze's rumour through corn.

Does the sea show anger?
Thumping waves, crashing breakers,
churning undercurrent?

Does a lake convey stoicism?
Silent shifts of depth,
reply, 'nothing's wrong',
when you know it is.

First published in *Obsessed with Pipework* #82, broadcast on BBC Solent, Feb 2020.

Hermit Crab
By Terry Dyson

last crouch made smooth
pearl ringed
mush'd against snug   rest long pincers
ring out peepers
sand shovell'd rude

moving out

un-shell   shally un-slick
along grittel
.Stalk Eyes.
dip small for plump down
shell domes to fit mound-full
my clacks   ~

beachcombers

shade legs snaffle up our opaque sleeks

shunt shell to ear-dangles   purring out oceans
hand raid our demigod designs
pinch switch our black bobble brines
.Stalk Eyes.
must scuttle link-quick-link-quick along

moving in

jack up shell-shape
orange purple nipper quince
      clip hustle
crundle twist slimp-scuttle
       inward   ~

Note: Hermit crabs line up to exchange shells when a new shell comes along.

I Throw my Anxiety into the Baltic Sea
By Thea Smiley

watch it arc over boulders, dark conifers,
over the wooden hut, the upturned boats,
over the ramshackle stones and galaxies
of starry moss around the Viking's grave.

It drops beyond the reflections of pines,
a splash that shatters the surface and sends
waves rolling across the expanse to strike
the reeds and rocky shores of the islands.

I picture it tumbling through water, far
from the lost fishing hooks by the jetty,
its weight dragging it into the sediment,
nosed by sticklebacks, needlefish and pike.

I think of it submerged, slowly corroding,
never to be dredged up or washed ashore,
trapped under snow and thick ice in winter,
a sunken hulk deep beneath the calm water.

Full Moon
By T W Warrpos

An unsettling calm rides the
tide, driven by
lunacy -
a cloud, bubbling over with magnificent rage,
nags the froth forming on furious crests as
the belly of the ocean erupts and spews
irritability, then
collapses, sobbing into the arms of the shoreline.

Untitled
By Vanessa Hope

dry with thirst
raindrops cupped
in a green leaf

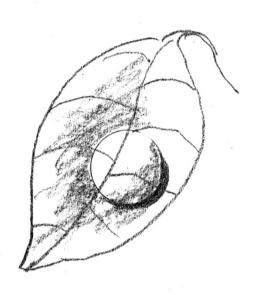

Acknowledgements

A huge thank you to...

all the poets in this anthology for trusting us with their words,

my co-editors, John Tessitore, Marc Brimble and Sarah Jeannine Gawthrop, for their hard work reading and selecting the poems for this collection,

Mike Curry for giving us permission to use his wonderful photograph,

Easkey Britton for taking the time to write a beautiful introduction on the theme of water,

Colin Thom for his fabulous illustrations,

Stuart Beveridge for his invaluable help with formatting, layout and design,

Katherine E Winnick for casting her beady eye over the manuscript,

and of course to you, dear reader, who holds this anthology in your hands, for purchasing a copy and for supporting a small press. Know that every penny of proceeds is donated to charity.

Claire Thom
EIC & founder of The Wee Sparrow Poetry Press

About The Wee Sparrow Poetry Press

Founded by Claire Thom in April 2022, The Wee Sparrow Poetry Press is an indie publisher which creates poetry anthologies and digital zines. 100% of the proceeds from sales of our anthologies is donated to charity. A small press with big ideas which aims to showcase fantastic poets from around the world, and give them a platform to get their words out there. The Wee Sparrow Poetry Press does not believe in charging submission fees and all the team are volunteers. We are a creative community trying to make wee ripples of kindness in a crazy world.

Email: theweesparrowpoetrypress@gmail.com
Instagram: @theweesparrowpoetrypress & @theweesparrowpoetrypodcast
www.theweesparrowpoetrypress.com

Other publications by The Wee Sparrow Poetry Press

Hope is a Group Project

An inspirational anthology of hope, featuring 98 international writers and original illustrations by Scottish artist, Colin Thom. All royalties are donated to charity.

To Live Here – a haiku anthology

A collection of haiku on the theme of home, which explores the many facets of human experience, from the mundane to the sublime. Featuring the work of talented poets from around the world, this anthology invites readers to reflect on the beauty and complexity of the world we inhabit. The original illustrations are by Scottish artist Colin Thom. All proceeds are donated to charity.

Our books are available globally on Amazon in paperback.

Still We Rise

A digital zine full of revolutionary poems reacting to the current state of the world, including original artwork by Colin Thom, Stuart Beveridge, Ally Zlatar and Jane Hanson. The zine is free to read online, just click the link on our website.

The poem, the song, the picture, is only water drawn from the well of the people, and it should be given back to them in a cup of beauty so that they may drink – and in drinking understand themselves.

~Federico García Lorca

Printed in Great Britain
by Amazon

37941570R00093